"Journey of a soul moving from darkness to Light."

LIVING IN LIGHT

"Journey of a soul moving from darkness to Light."

Zankhana

Invincible Publishers

Published by
Invincible Publishers
201A, SAS Tower, Sector 38, Gurugram - 122003
Phone: +91-124-4034247, +91 9355675555
www.i-publish.in

First Published in 2020
Copyright ©2020 Zankhana,
ISBN: 978-93-89600-69-8

Dedication

To you, Mom,

It's after losing you that I found myself;
one with God.

I dedicate this book to my mother, who had to leave me
physically, in darkness so that I could find
my way to living in light.

In spirit, she has always been there as my guiding light.

I dedicate this book to Dr. Wayne Dyer and Louis Hay,
whom I could not meet personally in this lifetime and
yet they have played a monumental role in my life by
inspiring me through their thoughts and works.

I also dedicate this book to YOU,
who has taken this step towards the light.

As you read this book may you be filled with his
Love and Light.

God Bless you.

ACKNOWLEDGEMENT

This book was never in my faintest dream. The writing of this book has been one of the greatest of all the miracles that you will come across in the following pages.

It was written in a few hours within 10-15 days. It is beyond my capacity as a human being and as a writer to do this by myself.

I am grateful to the core, to the Masters who chose me, to pour through me this divine guidance and wisdom.

With every word, every sentence, I feel I was renewed.

All the layers of me from lifetimes were shed in the process, until nothing of me remained, but HIS LIGHT.

I thank each and every person who has been a part of my life since I took my first breath, until now.

Each of the persons whom I have had contact with has only been my teacher in some way and has taught me some lesson in Life.

I truly thank my husband who has been a monumental support to me, from the day we met. He has loved me unconditionally always. We have had our dark times like every other couple but his faith in me and us, has always been like a tall mountain. I cannot thank him enough to have loved me and supported me like this throughout. I feel blessed to have him as my partner in this lifetime and I am so thankful to God for giving him to me.

I thank my two beautiful children who are the joys of my life. They are my Love and Light. These beautiful souls made me aware that God's light and love exists in me. Their coming in my life marked God's arrival in my world, and it changed me forever.

I would also like to thank my family on my in-laws' side, who is my support system. It is their love and support that makes the good days better and the tough days, easier.

I thank my father and brother and step mother for their unconditional love. I feel supported and nurtured by their presence in my life.

I am truly thankful to the Team Invincible, for their constant support and guidance, and for patiently holding my hand throughout the journey of bringing this book from concept to reality , in the best possible way.

I would also like to thank my dear friend, Janvi Mehta for helping me design the cover of the book. Through her creative talent and dedication she has splendidly re-created, my experience in the other dimension; one that will forever be close to my heart.

I thank God, the supreme Almighty, my Spiritual guide (Sai Baba), all the Spiritual Masters, Holy Gurus, all the Great Saints, and Guiding Angels.

I humbly thank Mother Earth.

I thank life, for expressing through me.

With Love and Light and in full faith,

Zankhana

INTRODUCTION

Hello Dear reader,

I would like to share with you in few words how this book came into light.

December 2019, when in one part of the world, the pandemic of Covid-19 had started spreading its darkness around the world, I was going through the most beautiful phase of existence.

I had arrived in the consciousness of supreme light. My long waited search for God had just ended, as I had found his light within the threshold of my closed eyes.

It had taken a series of struggles and heartaches and invincible faith for me to finally breakfree from the barriers of darkness in my mind and I was now basking in this divine light daily.

They said,

"We are a group of conciousness working to raise the conciuosness of the planet earth for better and easy transition to new era soon to arrive."

I was in awe of this message myself when I received it on 26th of December 2019. Only now as I go back to every message I received that it makes complete sense.

Now I know the releveance when time and again they insisted- "NO further delay. Do it now. Show up everyday. We need you to write a book."

Living in Light was written just as darkness had started to envelope the earth. At that time I had no idea why it was so important and urgent to write the book, but having had the sip of the nectare of divine communion I kept meditating everyday with discilpine and faith and as a result this book was written.

This book was written with a sense of urgency.

They insisted that I openly share every detail of my life with you, which ofcourse was not a very comfortable thing for me to do initially. However, with every passing day my communictaion with the Masters got better and they made me realise how important it is "To be the Truth" rather than just say the Truth.

Every word in this book is the Truth of my life. You are free to accept what you may like and leave the rest. However, I do insist that you must give yourself a chance to know God. There is so much power and bliss in is his love that instantly one can get free from all the clouds of darkness that rules our human-mind. You can find meaning in existence only when you realise who you truly are.

We have been conditioned to live in a particular way.

We have been conditioned to run after things that doesn't matter and in this chase we forget the main reason why we are here.

Social distancing was the only way through which the universe could break this chase of human beings for insignificant things.

I am sure that the lockdown, made each and ever person on this planet question his existence and meaning of life. Each soul has been moved at a consciuosness level by this Pandemic in some way or the other and thereby it has served its purpose.

It had been very long that someone had to put an end to this madness of chasing after grades and degrees and money, accumalation of material wealth, false power and instant gratifcation through various means.

This book is my humble effort to bring light in our world; that may seem to be filled with darkness today. Rest assure that penetrating through darkness, definitely will emerge out a light with such brilliance that it will lit up our world like never before.

Note : God is the father and the mother, God is worshipped in form and yet God is formless.

I would like to humbly bring to your notice that my use of "HE" for God is not gender specific, it is only and only to maintain a smooth flow of the language throughout the book.

You may worship God as divine father, divine mother, as Supreme Consciousness, as energy, or life force.

How each of us see God is absolutely our Personal choice.

Love and light,
Zankhana.

Contents

WHAT IS THE PURPOSE OF YOUR LIFE?

"Ask what is your purpose in Life and ask yourself why you have come here from so far. Be aware of the purpose of your coming here and strive for spiritual achievements."

- Mahavatar Babaji

Living in light is about how we can cross over and rise above the darkness; darkness in the form of fear, worry, stress, tension, anger, frustration and other negative emotions that seems to cloud our life and to learn to live life from light.

Today, we are living in an environment where we begin our life in a rush. Most of the time we are rushing through life. It is so easy for thoughts of negativity to make their way in our lives because of the lifestyle we have.

Living in light is about letting life flow through us and also an effort to stop us from rushing through life.

Living in light is about going from one moment to another, consciously. It is about knowing deep in our hearts that we are here for a purpose and that purpose is certainly not going to office, changing diapers, cooking or going to the movies and getting drunk and partying all night.

Each one of us gets stuck when we are asked the question–what is the purpose of our life?

We somehow seem to reach a dead end.

It is because we were never taught to live in the light. There is so much stress on good manners and behaviour, academic achievements and accumulation of material wealth but nobody ever taught us to think about the grander things of life.

Do you really think that you are born just to go to school and get a job and get married, have children, accumulate some wealth and die one day? Do you think that *this* is the purpose of your life?

This may be the general flow of life for a majority of people, but you don't live for the purpose of getting married, getting a job etc. With your age your purpose doesn't have to change.

So what do you think is the purpose of your life?

YOU ARE HERE TO CO-CREATE WITH GOD

"God is the Cosmic dreamer and we are the Co-dreamers with him"

- *Paramahansa Yogananda*

So, what is the purpose of our lives? The purpose of our lives is to expand our vision of life and to live everyday with this expanded vision.

The purpose of our lives is that we have to learn/realise that we have within us all the strength to bring to our real physical world, whatever it is that we desire to bring. This is what is needed to know that we are the CO-CREATORS with GOD.

Today, even science has acknowledged that there is a presence of a force that runs this whole show called life. I don't think I have to go on to explain that here.

I take it for granted that either you believe in that larger force or you will read about it in other places and come back here.

So, having believed that there is a presence that is all powerful and all knowing; we are still faltering in our thought about His presence.

Where we are mistaken is that we think that this force/this presence/this Spirit/God is outside of us.

It is not just outside us, it is all around us and most importantly it is within us.

The main purpose of life is to come to terms with and accept this fact that it is in the human heart that GOD /life force/spirit resides.

When we acknowledge this and live our day to day life with this knowledge, great things become possible. Miracles occur most naturally. Each miracle makes you feel stronger and stronger and then comes a time when miracles become a daily routine.

It is no nonsense that I speak here. I speak out of personal experience.

I will share in detail some of the miracles in my life in later chapters.

THROUGH OUR VIBRATIONS WE CREATE OUR WORLD

"If you correct your mind, the rest of your life will fall in place."

- Lao - tzu

Our heart beats in sync with the cosmic rhythm. With every beat goes out a vibration.

The vibration then reaches the cosmic centre and gets back to us in manifolds. I am sure each one of us has shouted out at the echo points of mountains at some time in your life. If not, do it next time you go to the mountains, without fail. This is exactly how it works in our lives too. The cosmos/universe echoes back to you the vibration you send out, in MANIFOLDS!

This is how miracles or disasters happen.

So, when you are sad and depressed, your heart beats in that frequency which is a low frequency and sends out a lower vibration, which returns back to you in manifolds. This is how things go from bad to worse or as a matter of fact they can go from good to best and happy to blissful.

The only way to break the cycle going from bad to worse is by changing the rhythm of your heart beats, which in turn can be changed by changing your thoughts. As thoughts have a direct effect on your heartbeats, energy follow thoughts.

How exhilarated you feel after dancing for half an hour or running or any physical exercise.

Your heart beats are faster, you may be physically exhausted but energy wise you are exhilarated, it's impossible for you to feel sad or depressed immediately after an hour of rigorous workout. You naturally feel good and high in spirit.

So good thoughts, positive thoughts make you feel light in energy and sad thoughts, negative thoughts make you feel heavier in energy.

When you are upset and you meet a friend who is in a high spirit, either you feel uplifted by the company or you feel extremely uncomfortable and leave soon and are stuck in that low energy field.

It is entirely our choice to which frequency we want vibrate in. Sometimes no matter how hard we try, we are unable to make that shift from low frequency thoughts to high frequency, we feel as if we are stuck. Thoughts can create havoc in human mind. This is when affirmations come to help. Have you heard of affirmations? Do you know what it is and how it works?

MAGIC OF AFFIRMATIONS

"We are what we think.
All that we are arises with our thoughts.
With our thoughts we make the world."

- Lord Buddha

Affirmations are positive statements made in present tense. They are the tool to change your frequency in thoughts, thereby, change in your vibrations. Change in vibrations will bring about change in your manifestations in life. It is magical how affirmations work.

I am love

I am Light

I am a Divine Being

I am a Powerful Being

I am Divine Health

I am Peace

I am Content

I am Blissful

How do you feel as you read these statements?

They may not be true at the point of time you are reading it. However, even reading them without them being true, makes you feel elevated.

Can you imagine how would you feel, if all these and other alike statements become the truth of your life? The power of affirmations is Paramount.

Since childhood we all are taught about how to sit, talk and behave, but somehow, we are never taught about how we should think. We are conditioned into classifications, that this is good, this is bad, don't talk like this, don't behave like this. When it came to the thinking process which is the base of how we behave and talk, we were never clearly taught about how we should be thinking all day long...

The fact is "we become what we think about all day long".

The common statements that generally we think are:

I don't know

I don't care

I am not sure

I am feeling low

I can't do that anymore

I am tired

I am fed up

I have no clue

I am all messed up in life.

How do you feel as you read these statements? You feel low and terrible.

You will say, but it is true about my life. Even if it is true about your life right now, wouldn't you like to change it around?

How can you change it if you continue to think the same and give out the same vibrations to the cosmos?

It doesn't know that you want to change it around, it only returns to you in manifolds what you send out.

So 'You' have a choice to break that pattern.

You must be aware of that story:

Two men in prison, one is looking out at the sky and the other looking down at the dust.

It is a Choice. It is entirely your choice to think that,

I AM DIVINE HEALTH or I don't know I am

feeling so sick.

Thoughts have an immediate effect on your body.

Then how do you change your thoughts?

By being conscious of everything you think.

By watching your thoughts constantly. By picking every negative thought and changing it into a positive one.

It will require some efforts initially but slowly you get into a habit.

I recommend each one of you to read the book,

"You Can Heal Your Life", by Louis Hay.

It is a book that changed me and my life entirely. Everything in my life was falling apart, (at least that is what I felt at that time), when I came across this book and believe me, this book transformed me.

There are so many tapes available on you tube on Affirmations. Just put on the affirmation tape at night as you go to sleep and let the powerful thoughts seep into your mind.

Soak your mind into affirmations every night. Initially, it may seem absurd, but trust me, you will see the result of that in 40 days and you will eventually feel the shift in your thoughts. You can also listen to them when in doubt or going through a difficult phase and it will make you feel lighter as they change your frequency while you are listening to them.

Affirmations work like prayers; I request you to include them in your routine. There are very few people today who would spend time in 'bhajan kirtan'; to connect to God.

Affirmation is a new age prayer to connect to God/Source/Spirit.

DARKNESS AND LIGHT ARE TWO SIDES OF THE SAME COIN

"The light shines in the darkness and the darkness has not overcome it"

- JOHN 1:5

Darkness is not separate from light, it is the flip side of light. In fact, everything in our life is just like that.

Each of us is constantly experiencing pain, happiness, sorrow, joy, success, failure in our day to day life. Earth is a planet of duality. In this duality lies the secret of the cosmos: that is, one is not separate from the other.

Joy and sorrow are two sides of the same coin. You cannot experience one without the other. All you have to do is just flip the thought to realise that both are two parts of the same coin. We must not want to avoid sorrow, because if we do that, we are left without both joy and sorrow! And what is life without a little joy and sorrow?

Only because there is night, we look forward to the day and vice versa. Can we imagine a world with only days or only nights?

Everything is designed in an intelligent way by the intelligent creator.

Even while we are aware of this nature of

duality; we still are unable to realise and live with this actual meaning and that is the major setback of life.

Somehow, in this duality lies the balance. Darkness and light together make the circle of life complete. It is when we come to understand this only then we can live our life without suffering. We suffer when we see or want to see only one side of the coin.

As soon as we become aware of this simple truth, our Life becomes as simple as this truth.

Next time when you are going through a dark patch of sorrow or failure or illness, you should know that all you need to do is flip the coin. Flip it by changing your thoughts about it. This will require absolute patience and faith. Patience and faith come with practice.

I will speak about it in next chapter.

ONLY BY BEING IN THE PRESENT, YOU LEARN TO BE PATIENT

*"There is neither Past nor Future.
There is only the Present."*

- *Ramana Maharshi*

We all have heard that patience is a virtue. Have you ever wondered why?

Let's try to flip it and see.

How do you feel when someone is constantly dealing with you impatiently?

Telling you the same thing 100 times in 10 minutes?

How do you feel when someone snaps at you, when all you meant was their good and well-being?

Now flip it again,

How do you feel when someone is all the time available for you; wants to hear you out completely with patience? When someone deals with all your emotional outbursts with kindness. Patience makes you feel loved and important. Impatience makes you feel unloved or less cared for.

Now go back to every moment in the recent past when you have acted out of impatience and see how you feel about it. Regret is what you feel, right?

Can you do anything about it now? Absolutely not!

Impatience will always find excuses, "people are always annoying, so I lost it!"

Again, impatience will always bring along its friend called, 'BLAME'.

Blaming others for your impatience is never justified. We all know that no matter how people behave, it is us, who always have a choice of how to react in any situation.

I have learnt this virtue and I am still learning from my most revered American author and public speaker, Dr. Wayne Dyer. He always said, whenever you have a choice to be right or kind, choose to be 'kind'.

Another important thing he said was, whenever you feel triggered and are about to lose your cool, just silently repeat these lines in your mind and you will cool it off.

"I choose PEACE, than this."

Patience is also about taking one step at a time and living one moment at a time. Most of us are so consumed by the desire of reaching the destination, that we completely forget to enjoy every step towards it and because we fail to enjoy and live completely every step of the journey to success, we feel empty when we finally arrive at it. And so again, we get desperate about what next now? This quench can never be met unless and until we do not recognise that the quench is not met at the destination but in every step of the journey.

In the process, a lot of time and experience goes unnoticed and unfulfilled.

Be in this moment.

Enjoy this moment. Live it to the fullest. Each moment is precious just like a heartbeat.

How does your heart beat when your two year old child comes running to you, how it stops for a second when he smiles at you and how together your heart beats when you both are enveloped in each other's loving embrace?

How just by looking into the eyes of someone, you can make contact with his/her soul. There is so much beauty and magic in each moment, no matter who you are, where you are, you can only feel this beauty and magic when you are completely in the moment.

Living with this awareness, enriches your experience of life. You may not realise it immediately, but when you look back after few years, would you want to smile or sigh at the days gone by?

So next time you are stuck in traffic or a red light, try and see the magic and beauty in that moment instead of losing your cool. Make a choice that will bring a smile to you and to people around you.

This comes only with practice. Start this right now.

As you read this, take a deep breath and feel every word you are looking at.

See how these words make you feel.

Slip in the words and let them sink deep in

your consciousness and see how your heart beats as you do this. Enjoy the rhythm of your pulsating heart.

Next time you are with your partner, children, co-workers, practice living in fullness of the moment.

Be one with that moment.

This is how you practice patience by being in the moment completely.

You will realise, you lose your cool only when you are not in this moment, either you are in the past or future.

Practice patience by being in the now!

FAITH IS THE ONLY WAY TO FREE YOURSELF FROM FEAR

"The whole secret of existence is to have no fear."

- Swami Vivekanada

When intellect fails, faith is born. When faith is born; intellect is subsided.

Faith and intellect, though they do not go hand in hand, they are the two sides of the same coin as well.

In our world, highly intelligent beings struggle to have faith. They can hardly acknowledge that there is some higher power. That's the supreme irony I feel. However, even the most intelligent beings when humbled with life's difficulties, after having struggled, do come to realise that there is something bigger than their intellect; and it is then that the seed of faith comes to fruition.

Faith is a belief not only in God, but a belief in your own self. Faith is not just a belief that God is outside us. But he is inside of you and everyone around you too.

Faith is believing in your own Godliness.

Faith is in knowing that you are a Divine Spark and you have the powers within you to Co-Create with God.

Often this faith comes after going through a lot of tests. Even after reaching this state of understanding and awareness, your faith is tested every now and then. With every test your faith reaches another level and makes you stronger and stronger. You become capable of doing extra ordinary things.

We are all born with the seed of faith in us. But when and how it sprouts to life, whether it is nurtured or lays there dormant for years, unnoticed, is all unique for each of us depending upon the environment we are born in.

Either we are taught to live in faith or fear. Living in faith is like jumping off a cliff, knowing that you will be taken care of, whereas living in fear is never wanting to let go off that cliff, surrounded with "what ifs?"

No matter what environment we are brought up in, one day we all have to reach a level where we learn to believe that everything will be taken care of.

It always has been that way.

Everything is in Divine right order, there are no mistakes in the Universe.

When we forge ahead in life with a heart full of faith, miracles are experienced, in most magnificent ways. As we progress on this path, more miracles occur and we become aware that we together with God can make miracles happen. The deeper the faith, the fuller and richer the experiences.

Life becomes larger than itself, when you live by faith. It requires for a strong mind and a lot of churning in that mind that finally leads you to attain this kind of faith.

It definitely comes with great difficulties, but the results are worth the pain.

Children who see their parents living with faith, become aware of the power of faith in the early stage of life. Faith comes easily when you are a child and not conditioned.

A child knows that his parents are always there and will take care in all situations. With time the child becomes independent and he starts feeling that he can survive on his own, and that he knows it all and has it all figured out. "It's my life" is what they think and no matter how much the parents love and want to reach out and protect their children, they have to watch them go through their own path and just be there watching and loving them.

No matter how much the distance and grievances may increase, one call from their child and the parents are ready to shower them with all their love.

It works the same way with God.

When we take birth, we feel now we are independent of God and it's our life. And we shun him out of our life, thinking that we can handle anything and that we know everything! But is that so?

True realisation and one genuine thought of him and he is ready to flow in and fill us with his love. Isn't it beautiful.

Most of our life passes by in living with fear and ego, unaware of this simple truth of life.

But each of us have to arrive at this stage of awareness and it is then that we learn to choose Faith over fear and ego.

We realise then, that the door to faith was always open. Only because we were filled with darkness of fear and ego, we never saw it. And now that we are in, we never want to look back.

POWER OF PRAYERS

*"If you become addicted to God,
then all your problems are solved. Go on
drinking the love of God,
until you become one with God.*

- Meher Baba

I read somewhere that prayer is when you talk to God and Meditation is when God talks to you. It is so true.

All prayers are always answered.

May it be of a better job, higher grades, larger house, better salary; it may take time but they are always answered. However, prayers for material things are answered in accordance to our own thought process and vibrations. But true prayer, that is when you are praying for strength, love, good health, peace, and that too when you are praying for someone else or your fellow beings; they are answered instantly. What we give out is what we receive. The most powerful prayer I have come across is the prayer by St. Francis of Assisi.

Prayer of St. Francis

Lord make me an instrument of your Peace,

Where there is hatred, let me sow Love.

Where there is injury, Pardon.

Where there is doubt, Faith.

Where there is despair, Hope.

Where there is darkness, Light.

Where there is sadness, Joy.

O Divine Master, Grant that I may not so much seek to be consoled, as to console;

To be understood, as to understand.

To be loved; as to love.

For it is in giving that we receive,

It is in pardoning, that we are pardoned.

And it is in dying that we are born to Eternal life.

Each time I read this prayer I am moved to the core. It is so simple and beautiful and summarises all the prayers in one.

Praying fills us with strength and yet it is so sad that when all fails, it is then that man feels the need to pray.

We may believe in him or not, but we end up praying one day when everything seems to fail.

It is the ego that believes that "I can do everything".

But we are mistaken.

We cannot put breath in a dying person, he can!

We cannot make a flower bloom, he does!

We cannot bring the sun to rise, he does!

We cannot even mend our car, but he mends the life of thousands every day.

How can we not believe in the power of the creator, while we see it in every smallest thing all around us.

How can we be so driven by our ego that we fail to see the simplest truth of life?

How do we explain the coming in of the breath and going out of it, in our body?

Can we guarantee that there will be the next breath coming?

Are we the one handling it?

We do not control our own breath, how do you think the universe works?

It is beyond human understanding.

Then why not accept him and pray?

Why do we have to wait for prayer to be our last resort? Why not make it our daily resource?

With prayers you build a relationship with God either of a friend or parent. When you nurture that relationship with prayers every day, you will see how it is not a one-way street, that it is not an unrequited love either. He will love you back and you will feel his love envelopes you, moves you and makes you realise your own magnificence.

Soon you will realise that you and him are not different, that You are One.

You and all the beings are ONE.

We are so humbled by prayers and yet we refuse to pray because of ego. This ego is nothing but a darkness of ignorance. We need to bring in Light (light of new thoughts) to remove the darkness.

So, let us bring in the light through knowledge, new thoughts, prayers and faith.

Like mentioned earlier, all we need to do is just flip the coin.

So, let us bring in the light through knowledge, new thoughts, prayers and faith.

Like mentioned earlier, all we need to do is just flip the coin.

I would like to end this chapter with a quote by Mother Teresa

If we pray, we will believe;

If we believe, we will love;

If we love, we will serve.

MEDITATION

*"Your ability to fly
in the inner world,
depends upon
Your ability to forgive others."*

- Master Chao Kok Sui

There are so many ways to meditate these days. It really makes me happy with the kind of awareness that have spreaded lately, across the world for the need to sit still and look within. More people are willing to adopt meditation in their routine.

Meditation is like sitting at the ocean and watching each wave come and go with stillness. Once you do that for long you become one with the ocean and each wave. And all differences fade away.

Similarly, when you meditate every single day upon the stillness you become the stillness, the Peace.

If you meditate upon love, you become Love.

When you meditate upon God, you realise that you and him are one and there is no separation whatsoever. You merge in him and start living your day to day life with him. This is how you become truly God- realised.

Now you are not just aware of your Oneness with him, but you are also able to act and live with this Oneness with all, which you never experienced earlier.

Loving and accepting people becomes easy, rather natural.

Anger, hatred, fear, anxiety, worry all cease to exist.

You live in bliss and you become one with each moment. You are no longer rushing through life rather you feel, you are flowing in perfect rhythm with life.

People are simply attracted to you and they love being in your presence.

It doesn't bother you to give love.

The more you give, the more love you feel oozing out of you.

This all sounds fictitious but believe me it is true and many people have experienced this truth. This is the truth of my life too.

When I look back, I see what I was 15 years ago and what I am now. People around me have also witnessed this process of my growth, from being restless to blissful.

The road was treacherous and every step felt like a mountain.

But with faith and prayers I trod on, didn't even realise when and how meditation became a way of my life.

I was in complete surrender and let God take over the control of my life.

He filled me with peace, love, strength and grace.

Today, I am so humbled by his love and presence that all I can and want to do is sing his praise with every breath I take.

If I can be so enveloped in his love, so can you. Rather, I would say 'So are you'!

Just become aware and take one step towards his Light and all the Darkness will fade away.

There are many ways to feel God's presence. But if you want to feel him like a companion, talk to him on a daily basis, share with him your little worries.

I suggest you meditate every day.

If you promise to show up, he definitely will!

MAGIC AND MIRACLES

"In the light of calm and steady awareness, inner energies wake up and work miracles without any effort on your part."

- Nisargdatta Maharaj

Once we have changed our path from Darkness towards Light, once we start acting with patience and faith; every moment, every day seems magical as you experience many miracles.

Magic and Miracles are nothing but events that occurs in such synchronicity, that it leaves you completely spell bound and you feel ecstatic about everything happening around you.

This happens when you have raised your thoughts and awareness to a level, where you are constantly living with oneness, oneness with God and oneness with all.

It is like after having been through a dark thundering, lightening night you wake up to a glorious sunrise with a beautiful rainbow.

Miracles happen with the shift in your thoughts, it is an inward experience. That is why miracle is what some people experience every day and yet some fail to see anything miraculous at all.

Miracles become a routine for the ones who makes God (no.1) their Routine.

Every day, every moment seems magical then. It is just that you are living from a higher consciousness now.

This is my personal experience. Once I shifted my thoughts from "me to we",

(Me- me alone, separate from God

We- me together, hand in hand with God)

everything about my life changed.

When I realised that my life is nothing but a journey towards him; every step of the journey became easier.

Every step became fascinating.

Every test/difficulty seemed momentary.

I knew I could handle anything now that I feel one with him.

The journey to God is the purpose of each one's life.

But the sad part is we realise this only after going through a lot of pain, struggle and frustration. The realisation takes most of our life, and yet there are some who spend their lifetime until they realise this.

I strongly believe this can be changed. People can be saved from a lot of frustration, unnecessary pain and cycles of negative-dark emotions.

The objective of this book – 'Living in Light' is to spread awareness that life is not a struggle, it is not so painful that we wish to discontinue this struggle.

It is not a meaningless time pass affair either.

We are not here just to go to school or office, get married and procreate.

Rather, it is a beautiful experience where God wants to live through us.

We are his senses.

Just like you experience a good movie through your eyes, heart, brain and just like you taste your food, with mouth, tongue, teeth.

He is experiencing his creation through each one of us.

We are his hands, mouth, feet, eyes.

We are Him. He is Us.

He cannot completely experience his creation until each one of us realises that 'We are him and He is Us'! That we are One with him and that we are all ONE.

Just like we feel discontented, he too feels discontent until all his fragments (us) realise their divinity, their power.

Each one of us can co-create with God, everything that we want to.

Since we are him, we have all his powers.

We have his capacity to Love one and all,

We have his capacity to Forgive one and all.

We have his capacity to bless one and all.

We are Peaceful and Magnificent like him.

We are Divine beings living life to realise our own Divinity.

God is Light.

We are his Light.

Darkness is but just an illusion, it is nothing

but the absence of Light.

When we realise that we are his Light, all the darkness fades away.

God is Love.

We are his love.

Fear is absence of Love.

When we realise that we are His Love, all the fears fade away. As we realise this and live our life with Light and Love, we become One with Him and one with all.

To realise this Oneness and to live in this Oneness is the real Purpose of each and everyone's life.

MY JOURNEY TOWARDS GOD

"It is better to see God in everything
than to figure it out."

- *Neeb Karoli Baba*

How it began?

Just like a plant has to go through various stages to grow into a Tree; my journey towards God has been long. The seed of love was planted when my Mother conceived me. I have heard from my father and other family members that it was my mother's deep desire to have a girl when she was pregnant with me, as I have one elder brother before me. She must have prayed really hard to have a daughter. Her prayers were answered as I was born and so, instantly I was named–Zankhana–meaning a strong desire (in this case for a baby girl) in Gujarati language.

My journey to God initiated with the loss of my mother when I was 10 years old. Back then, I had no clue that I could ever see a silver lining behind the darkest cloud of my life.

I had a very tough childhood. I have no clue about how I grew up without the soul of the family. Now being the mother of two myself, I understand that a mother is truly the soul of the family.

I remember the exact scene when my mother

left this world to progress on her journey in eternity.

12TH October 1994, it was the eight night of Navaratri. My mother, a devotee of Shakti, usually observed fast for nine days of Navaratri. But this time she couldn't as she was not very well. She had been complaining of chest pain since last few days. All the reports were normal. The doctor concluded that the pain was a result of indigestion issues. That day she was very much in pain so we had called the doctor home to check her. The ECG was normal so, the doctor left and my father and brother went to drop the doctor and get some medicines. My paternal grandmother was finishing up the kitchen's work and I was sitting with my mother as she lay down in pain, suffering from something that was not being traced.

She felt the urge to vomit and so she went up to the bathroom. I helped her, holding her hand as she rushed to the bathroom. I massaged her back as she vomited and called my grandmother.

But before my grandmother came into the room, my mother while walking back towards the bed, suddenly fell down on the floor. I managed to hold her head in my lap and just like that she left. One moment she was here and the next she was gone. I saw her breathe her last breath. At that moment she was liberated, but I got caged in the trauma of losing her. It took me 15 years to free myself from the shackles of the pain of that one moment.

Soon after losing her began my relationship with God, my invisible eternal friend. My journey toward God has seen five main seasons. With every passing season I moved closer to God. I share this Beautiful journey with you, hoping it will bring you some comfort if you are going through difficult times and wishing that you do not give up on your search for him, because trust me, the night seems the darkest and longest , just when the dawn is near and the sun is about to rise. Hang in there and you will find him waiting to melt you in his love and grace.

SEASON OF FRIENDSHIP

"*The divine has loved me as mother, as father, and as friend, behind all friends. I searched for that one friend behind all friends, that one lover whom I now see glimmering in all your faces. And that friend never fails me.*"

- *Yogananda*

What followed after my mother's passing away was chapter after chapter of difficulties, pain, isolation and depression. I felt weird from the rest of the children of my age, I felt deep loneliness and that I do not belong here. I couldn't connect with anybody. Everybody saw me with pity and not love. I felt starved for love and attention. There was no goal, nothing to do. Every day as if was a punishment, every breath; a burden. I felt so heavy, as if I was carrying a huge burden. And yet for the sake of my father and brother, I faked a happy face. The more I pretended to be normal, the more miserable I felt. But I couldn't break the loop of sadness and pretension of being happy. I felt so helpless.

Bathroom was my favourite place to cry. People teased me for being in the bathroom for several hours. Little did they know what happened behind the door and among the bathroom walls. Somehow those walls made me feel safe and became my best friends, who never judged me for being so weak. I constantly prayed for strength and help.

There were some nights when I went up to the terrace and yelled and cried, when the pain was unbearable and during one of those dark nights, I came across God. I don't remember what exactly had triggered me that night, I just remember that the pain I felt was so unbearable that I cried and complained and summoned God, that either you go through this pain along with me or free me of this pain. I cannot take it any longer.

Nothing happened that night. I just remember I had fallen asleep crying.

But the next day, I felt a strange calmness enveloped me.

I was filled with hope and cheer. It was weird. Until that day I had been in fighting and complaining mode, but somehow that day I felt as if I had reconciled with God and life.

I apologised for being so mad at him. I felt I could move ahead with him by my side. And that day I made friendship with God. I started talking to him about every single thing. I was constantly in dialogue with him, wherever I was. He became my best buddy. Life became better as I felt lighter in thoughts. I smiled a true smile, when I laughed, I laughed genuinely. Being honest with my feelings made me feel good. I started wondering about deeper facts of life; who am I? Why I am here?

Slowly and slowly (gradually), my thoughts expanded and I started feeling one with everyone who was going through a difficult time or pain. While children of my age would play in the recess time at school, I would look around for kids who were sad or upset over things and would cheer them up. It gave me happiness to bring a smile on someone's face or to comfort someone.

Eventually, I made good friends. I loved them and cared for them deeply. It brought me discomfort whenever my friends had a disagreement among themselves over something and I always tried to cease fire and spread only love. I was still young to recognise what was happening. There were tough days, days when feelings of loneliness would take over, but I shared with my buddy (God) and somehow, I came around easily with little pains of life.

My relationship with my dad and brother had deepened after losing mom. January 1998, my brother left the city in pursuit of his dream, of becoming an actor. Only my father and I supported him for this,the rest of the family was extremely against this idea. However, what mattered to him most was that my father and I, was on his side. So, he went on in the direction in which his heart led him.

He made a huge leap in one years' time, he was on T.V. He became my hero, he always was, being 6 years elder to me. But now he inspired me. I felt extremely proud of him and I thanked my Buddy- God to have supported and taken care of me and my family.

I had developed a strong intuition. I always knew when there was trouble around the corner. I was protective of people I cared for. Often I travelled alone to Mumbai (to my maternal family), alone. I would intuitively know if there were some kind of danger or strange people around and my intuition helped me protect myself and stay safe. I felt someone protecting and guiding me all the time.

In 1999, my father remarried. I was 15 years old and had turned into a somewhat rebellious teenager. Of course, I was not psychologically in a stage to accept someone else as my mother. But my brother convinced me that it was for the betterment of our father. I didn't understand that. But today I realise how important it is to have a life partner, to share the pain of the struggles of life and to celebrate the joys of life.

My reluctance to accept her as my mother, brought in only tough times for the family. This I say and realise now, but back then I only blamed life and others for my sufferings or struggles with my step-mother.

Once again, I got into complaining mode, became bitter and aggressive. The more I became bitter the farther I felt from God. I felt rejected by him and I started blaming him for it. I felt distant from him and so sought company in other friendships. Fortunately, I was blessed with good friends with whom I still share a wonderful bond of friendship. I had few friends and I still have the same friends today. I see it as a good thing. Friendships made in childhood are very special, as the foundation of those friendships is pure and innocent. There are no expectations in such friendships except that of love and care. As I felt abandoned by my buddy - God I resorted to my friends for cribbing and blaming the world and people in my life. I think it is the teenage that aggravated my emotions.

After a year my brother got married, and intuitively I knew that life is about to change 360 degrees for us as a family and it did. The same year my father went through some financial loss and life got more and more complicated with every passing day.

I felt so frustrated with dad's mood swings and step mother's behaviour towards me that I decided to shift to Mumbai in 2003 on my brother's insistence, and much to my father's disagreement. Intuitively, I was not at all comfortable with the idea myself, but I was so upset with the situation at home that I decided to forge ahead. I left for Mumbai with the fear of uncertainty and much to my father's disappointment. He was very saddened by my choice but I was unstoppable in teenage aggression.

From the day I decided to shift to Mumbai nothing seemed to be in sync with life, instead everything got more and more complicated with each day, including my relationship with my brother, father and other relatives. I was in the second year of my college then. After a few days in Mumbai, I realised that either I had to repeat the First year of college or take a drop from college and do some diploma course as it was against the rule to change state university in the middle of Graduation. I was totally shattered as I was very interested in English Literature and dreamed to go abroad for further studies after graduation.

After a month in Mumbai, I did realise that my

decision of coming was proving to be wrong in all sense, practically and emotionally. My father could sense it and comforted me that I could always return back home. The more kindness he showed to me, the greater ego, I felt about not wanting to go back as a loser. I was adamant that I would stick to my decision and prove that it was a right thing to do. That I knew better. This is what ego does to you. It blinds you so much that even if you practically see a pit just infront of you, you wouldn't accept it unless you fall into it.

As days passed, and my situation worsened, practically and emotionally.

I felt I had messed up everything big-time my relationship with my dad, my brother, my education and people seemed to just bully me, as a matter of fact I felt I was bullied by life. I felt like a sunken ship. No ray of hope or any direction. I felt like a complete disaster. I loved my dad and brother the most and because of me they were put against each other. The two people who I loved dearly and whose well-being was my only desire, life had put them against each other and I had already ended up hurting them both and yet I was asked to make a choice between them. How could I ever make such a choice? I loved them both. I felt so torn apart between them.

I was just 17 and thought that I was just incapable of making such a choice.

It was my immaturity and negativity that had created this huge bubble of Negativity which was suffocating, so suffocating that all I wanted to do was to miraculously escape this bubble. But, how?

I didn't have the courage to break my brother's heart, and tell him that though, I loved him endlessly, I didn't trust him completely after his marriage.

I didn't have the courage to apologise to my father for my egoist behaviour. I felt so guilty and abashed by my past behaviour with him. He had been so unconditional in giving love and I had been so selfish and self centred.

I didn't have the strength to face my step-mom after being so intolerant to her. I didn't have the strength to be judged by my relatives.

I didn't have the courage to look into the mirror and face myself, or face my buddy–GOD. I realised that; I had chosen blame over him, I had chosen bitterness over him, I had chosen anger over him, I had so lost myslef in my ego- that I had edged- God (my buddy) –out.

In my heart though I knew I was in a mess that I couldn't get out without his help, I felt, I didn't deserve his help. I felt so guilty. I felt like a criminal. I had broken hearts; I had brought war in place of love. I had brought so much pain to the two people I loved the most and who loved me the most. I had failed my mother. I had failed God. I felt so miserable and so guilty.

So, I took the way of a coward. I tried to commit suicide. Standing in front of the mirror, I attacked myself with reasons why I didn't deserve to live anymore; not realising the absurdity of what I was about to do. Not realising that, all I had to do then was just surrender and ask for help.

So, lost *I* was in the darkness of the Ego, *I* didn't seek help from anyone or God and *I* decided to end my life, thinking that *I* could end all my struggles. Thinking that *I* could erase all my blunders, *I* took sleeping pills with tears in my eyes and slept off.

I was too depressed in life to take such a decision. I was just 17. And though nobody held me guilty, I felt responsible for everything that had went wrong in our life as a family and the relationship that had turned sour. Of course I was not the only one to be blamed for it. It was all about the choices all of us made as a family as we went through some tests of life.Even if one of us would have made a different choice, the situation would have been different.

I see lot of divorce cases happening these days, and my heart goes out to children of seperated families. They may not show it , but they definitely suffer. At a subconscious level they feel responsible for the seperation of their parents, and desperately wish their world was not broken. They are constantly battling with insecurity and helplessness. Such children if they are not healed and attended to at the right time, become victims of depression in later years of their life.

When we are going through depression, we find ourselves as victims; victims to life, victims to people, victims to situations of life. We feel we are shut in a suffering box and there is no key to that box. It suffocates you, but neither your life ends nor your suffering seems to end. Some people at this point lose it, and take extreme steps thinking that they can end this suffering and free themselves and some people make suffering their friend and continue suffering all their lives, making other people suffer with them too.

Today everyone is combating with depression in their life. I think it is like a mental flu. We keep getting it once in a while and it is contagious too. While some people acknowledge it, some people don't, some people pretend to be strong, some people are indeed strong, but most people are fearful and scared of being judged.

People who acknowledge being depressed, are the people who can easily come around it, rather than people who out of fear don't acknowledge it.

The key to open that box you are trapped in, is within yourself. Instead of feeling like a victim, only when you see within yourself, you come across your own frailties that arise from being weak minded.

All of your weaknesses are the flip side of your strengths. But you can access flip side only by surrendering to your higher self, your sacred self which knows that YOU are a part of God. Just like a drop of the ocean is a drop and yet it has all the qualities of the ocean. Each one of us is a part of God having all his attributes.

Realise that you are not your weakness, you are not your thoughts, you are not your body, you are not your judgements, but you are an eternal being.

When you realise, that you are a Divine being,

having a human experience to understand and realise your divinity, it is then that you feel free from all the limitations and sufferings.

Know that you are all powerful, all loving and all kind and that you are here not to suffer but to BE YOUR BEST VERSION.

This world was not created so that we suffer and seek God's help for liberation. This world is the result of the innumerable choices we make as individuals and as groups, given the complete freedom of will, by God. It is not "HE", who is making us suffer through the crimes and all the negative things that we see in the world. It is our choices that we make as individuals and as collective. We suffer because of the choices we make. At any point of time, things can be changed for better or worse, by making a different choice.

It is my insistence to you, dear reader, to choose light, to choose love, to choose God. I have done so and so I say, choose to live in the light.

I apologise for my detour from the story. I felt it was necessary.

Though I planned to end my sufferings, God made me realise that I was getting out of track on the original plan that I had signed up for and I was saved. I slept as a weak egoist me but woke up as a strong and surrendered person. For days after that I was in slumber as to what had happened. I got so quiet and numb that people were scared of and with me. They must be having innumerable thoughts of worry for me from that day on, but I lost all my worries since that day.

I became God-led. I am truly grateful that God saved me and gave me yet another opportunity to realise the value of this human life.

For many days, I tried to remember what happened, and make sense of it. I just couldn't remember anything. As if someone had put the whole episode into a trash bin and pressed refresh, after it.

Something in me had definitely changed.As after that incident difficulties never ended, but I became more resilient to everything that came on my way.

SEASON OF
LOVE AND FAITH

*"The winds of God's grace are always blowing,
it is for us to raise our sails."*

- Swami Ramkrishna

It is then in December 2003, that I met Punit- My husband. The way we meet and the way we connected and became best of friends is a divine orchestration. It will take me to write a whole book on how we met and how we became partners on this Journey to God.

We enjoyed a good friendship for 3 years and then got married. There were some family struggles as we belonged to different castes. But if the love is true, everything is resolved. And most of all it was a divine plan for me and Punit to join in this organisation called Marriage to begin our Journey to God.

Until then we both were on and off in our relationship with God. He was more on the side of an atheist, whereas I had always felt this invisible companionship with God. Punit was intrigued with my past and he was convinced that some divine power had been taking care of me.

Soon after we united in marriage, we came across a very spiritual and Divine being, Sai Ma. She was instrumental in initiating our spiritual journey. She is a devotee of Shirdi Sai Baba. We came in touch with her through my cousin. My sister went to Sai Ma's place regularly where there was a small temple. They very lovingly and religiously did Pooja, Aarti and Abhishek of Sai Baba and other deities there. Both me and Punit were very new to the idea of religious worship then. But we were open-minded and somehow, we were very attracted to Sai Ma, who reflected divine love and kindness in hercountenance. Through her guidance we started our spiritual journey by reading about Sai baba- Sai Sat Charitra(The life and teachings of Sai Baba) and doing rituals like aarti, pooja and kirtan with pure desire to know him. Slowly we started feeling his presence in our life. Little synchronicities like coming across more of Sai devotees randomly, coming across Baba's pictures wherever we went, on rickshaw, on the bus, on poles on the road. These little little things added to our quest to seek him more. We became regular and disciplined in our prayers. We developed faith bit by bit knowing more about him, experiencing his subtle presence in our life. As we practised Faith, belief came naturally to us, in the miraculous healing power of prayers and his udi(ash). On one hand, the drama of life continued, the daily struggles of family life, business life, adjustment issues in a new culture; and on the other hand, we got more and more inclined towards God.

The spiritual thirst made us read books and we realised that in the most difficult times, our faith increased. I specifically started depending more on Sai Baba. His name itself melted me with so much love. I find myself incapable of completely expressing my love for him. I was very young and I had too many questions. It was difficult for me to except the things and people as they were. Because I was so filled with his love, it baffled me why everyone could not feel this love. If only people could see his love and grace, all the worries in the world would end. My limited mind was limiting me from a higher perspective, that I have today. We also took guidance from Sai Ma, many times as later we realised that it was her pure love for

Saibaba that she had also become " medium" to help people.

She did auto-writing and guided many people. We were so awed by this experience of how she would connect to Baba and automatically the messages flowed through her pen. The messages were clearly divine. I secretly wished, if only I could become so pure in my devotion that Baba would flow through me like he did with Aunty. I would love to be of service to mankind. The whole process of connecting to Sai Baba through automatic writing and through aunty as a medium, changed our life and perspective about being able to reach God. The belief that God resides somewhere up in heaven and is unreachable was transformed into an idea that he is very reachable through prayers and guidance through mediums. This is when we came across this book, *The Laws of the Spiritual World by Khorshed Bhavnagri.*

As I felt this strong devotion to Sai Baba, many things happened in the background of my life. My father was going through a very rough time and also my brother's relationship with my father was getting more strained. My brother had completely cut off from me after I had returned back to Ahmedabad in 2003. He did surprisingly come to my wedding and played his role as a brother and we had few magical moments of love and reconciliation as a family. However, after my wedding he again disappeared completely from our lives.

I had a feeling he was going through a storm in his personal life as well, but he wouldn't speak at all about his struggles so I left it to God. Every day I prayed for him and my father. I had deep faith that someday all will be well and it will be very beautiful.

While all the chaos went on in the background, what surfaced was the love for God and day by day increasing faith in him. Fortunately, Punit and I felt the same way about our love for God. We had a difficult two years of our life as a married couple, with a lot of expectations, dis-satisfactions, ego battles, dis- agreements on almost everything. But when it came to Love for God, we were always on the same page and it is because of this love for God, forgiveness came to us easily.

It was very easy for him to forgive and let go after every tiff we had. But for me, while forgiveness came easily, I found it extremely difficult to let go and move on. I held on to the pain of the hurt and I suffered.

There was a part of me which was deeply frustrated with the useless fights and dis-harmony in life and relationships with people around me, *but that part of me also resorted to God for everything instead of taking everything to ego and getting back at* people. Love for God had made me a peace lover, I could forgive people easily but when it came to Punit, I held on to the pain. This led to more stressful relationship. I had too much of expectation from him as a partner. I expected him to see life, as I saw it. It was difficult for me to accept him the way he was and I kept putting my expectations for him to change and in the process, I got frustrated. As nobody can change anybody. We can only make efforts to change our self, which also is an arduous task.

I was aware of my frailties and I prayed to God to help me with my flaws. Help us stay and live in harmony.

I now realise how naïve and insensitive it is to expect anybody to see life the way you see it. Most of the time we are oursleves so unclear about things in our own head, that it is so unjustified to expect somebody to think and feel the way we do or want them to.

Afterall, each of us have our own path to reaching the same destination (God).

SEASON OF PATIENCE

"Patience can be larger, bigger,
Brighter than you know.
It heals, it helps, it gives unexpected results to
Every unusal storms."

- Swami Vivekanada

In early 2008, I got pregnant and I was in some divine frenzy. It was a very smooth pregnancy, my gratitude and devotion for Sai Baba was raised to another level through this pregnancy. I spent most of the time in prayers, listening to kirtans and reading Sat-Charitra of Sai-Baba, eating healthy food, avoiding outside food and negative t.v. shows. Only prayers and singing his praise gave me joy. Throughout pregnancy, in spite of the background chaos I found myself enjoying the new phase of life, of living in love with my God and my Guru- Sai Baba.

At the end of pregnancy there were some complications. I had developed high blood pressure and my doctor had suggested that we go for a C-section instead of taking the risk of natural delivery.

Being a true Sai Baba devotee now, it was the time for the test of our Faith (Shraddha) and Patience (Saburi), The two lessons Baba says are must to learn in life to reach God. Both me and Punit were prepared for this test. We decided to wait for natural birth, having faith that all will be well and Sai-Baba will take care of me and the baby. The day my daughter was born was the day our faith had transcended to another level. It was a 12-hour labour with 6 hours of intense labour and I was losing patience by the end. It is then that Punit, gave me strength and started reciting the prayer Sai mahima aloud. Sai mahima is a 14-verse prayer like Hanuman chalisa. It gives strength and has great healing powers if one does it with faith.

As he held my hand, he recited Sai mahima – Something miraculous happened, I stopped crying in pain as if Baba took over me, my body, my pain, my labour. I didn't cry at all for 15 mins till Punit finished reciting it. It was out of the world experience. As I have completely no memory of those 15 mins of my life; as if I was not a part of this word for those 15 mins. Soon after the completion of Sai mahima, the doctor confirmed that I would be delivering naturally soon. Scientifically the cervix that had not dilated even 1cm in 11 hours, had dilated 8cms in 15 mins. It was a miracle.

Even the doctor and all the nurses were moved by this experience and acknowledged the Grace of God that we had felt.

The joy of devotion, the victory of faith and patience we felt, surpassed all the other joys of life we had ever felt.

We named her Bishakha as that was the name given to us through auto writing. We thanked Baba through Sai Ma and insisted that he suggest a name for our daughter, who was indeed his beloved daughter and his precious gift to us. We celebrated this miracle of faith and patience and it got engraved in our soul.

Life became very delightful and joy filled as little Bishakha grew. Her smile warmed our hearts and her little mischiefs brought us joy. She brought light into our world. Loving Sai Baba came naturally to her. I remember when she was 5 years old, Punit tried to teach her to read Sai mahima. I thought she was too young to read hindi but to my surprise she could read Sai mahima from the book in third attempt. Punit read it out to her twice and the third time she could read by herself. It is amasing how children learn things when they are in mother's womb. We stress a lot these days to take care of needs of a new born, I think equal care should be taken when the mother is pregnant. Apart from the food and exercise its is also important that the expecting mother reads, listens and speak and also learn good things. Again I say this out of personal experience.

Years passed and with the passing time, as we progressed in our curriculum of faith and patience, new chapter was added in the course of divinity: Surrender.

SEASON OF SURRENDER

"Why fear?
When I am here."

- Sai Baba

Outer world got more chaotic, so much so that it started having deep impact on our inner well-being. On one side the situation between my father and brother worsened, I almost thought that I had lost my brother forever. The struggles of Life had snatched him away and I was deeply affected with this pain.

On the other hand, me and Punit felt disconnected because of the outer environment of our life, impacting me deeply. I started losing control over my mind, frustration led to anger, anger led to guilt, guilt led to depression and fear of expressing clutched me. I created a wall around me of these negative thoughts that unfortunately blocked God's love to reach me.

Though I continued to pray, I prayed more in desperation than in faith. The vibration that I gave out was of desperation and not love.

However, once you surrender to the Master, you may give up on the master, but he never gives up on you.

I was battling with depression once again.

Most of the days I felt numb, like a lifeless body. Just going about the day mechanically, as if nothing mattered. Nothing brought joy to me, not even my child. Instead there were times that Bishakha became the victim of my frustration, realisation of which made me sink further deep into the whirlpool of guilt.

I have realised that fear and guilt are the most negative, sticky energy to get rid of. Their clutch is so strong that without the grace of a Guru it feels like an inconceivable task. Only when one surrenders all his emotions and weakness to God and let go of the need to control completely; it is then that the new chapter begins.

My relationship with Punit struggled as I once again had started falling prey to the vicious cycle of negative thoughts.

He had always been a supporting husband more like a sibling or a friend, of course we had our own failings as husband and wife but yet he had that maturity to see and act beyond the roles we played. He genuinely desired to help me get a better understanding of myself and a hold over my emotions. It always stressed him that I was over sensitive about relationships that mattered to me. I expected more and so I was affected more in relationships that I cared about.

Also, lately, I had been alienating myself from family and friends. He could see I was drowning more and more in depression. The thing that bothered me most was that I felt I was falling in the trap of repeating the pattern of my mother's life. She had a similar thought process just a few years before she passed away. As a child I had seen her go through depression which I didn't understand then, but I could relate to it now. The more I could relate to the memory of her, I started having thoughts of death. I was consumed with the fear that I too would die like my mother, leaving behind Bishakha. There were days when I could see the absurdity of my thoughts, but there were also days when I was totally engulfed by this fearful thought and thinking about what would happen to Bishakha after me, broke my heart.

I was not afraid of death but I didn't want my child to go through what I had gone through. The fear seemed so real somedays, that it drove me insane. Yet there were days when I was absolutely normal. There was a constant battle going on between one side of me that would succumb to the dark thoughts and the other side of me that had faith and was desperately praying to be in light. I kept praying to God to help me deal with this difficult phase of my life. But with my negativity I had blocked his light from flowing to me.

At that time, I was reading the book *Many lives, many Masters by Dr Brain Weiss.* I have always been intrigued with death and past life regression. Suddenly, I felt the need to go for past life regression. So, I looked for the hypnotherapist in Ahmedabad and I found none. I booked an appointment with a well known doctor/hypnotherapist in Mumbai.

I was very nervous before the session; however, I had an intuition that I was led there. I took a leap of faith and went ahead with the session.

My experience of past life regression, opened another dimension of reality to me. Technically what they do in past life regression is that the therapist calms your physical body and conscious mind through suggestive relaxation technique, as a result subconscious mind comes to the fore and the conciuos mind takes the back seat just like it happens every night while you sleep. Then with the permission and guidance of your spiritual guide, your awareness is guided to those part in your subconscious mind that holds the memory of all the lifetimes and the in-between periods between the lifetimes. It takes you to the most relevant lifetime where you are energetically stuck and due to which you are facing certain problems in the present life.

So once the therapist relaxed my physical mind and body, she asked me to focus on each word that she spoke and with her words she guided me to take my awareness to a plane of consciousness where I would find my spiritual guide waiting for me.

I felt the awareness as a spinning ball. It went far somewhere in space, while I was just lying there on her couch. After having felt going upward for a while I(my awareness) reached a place where all I saw was darkness for a short while and then slowly penetrating through the darkness, emerged a striking golden and white light. It spreaded all around me and I found myself engulfed in that powerful white light. As the light got less intense I found myself in front of a huge banyan tree. From behind the banyan tree appeared a figure in white, as I tried to focus on the figure to recognise it, I realised it was my Guru- Sai Baba. I was in shock and surprise and I could hardly believe my eyes. I had always craved for Baba's Darshan and yet never thought in my wildest dream that it was actually ever possible.

So overwhelmed I felt by his presence I bursted out in tears of gratitude and ecstasy. He opened his arms and I rushed into his loving embrace. His warm embrace and ever-loving smile instantaneously melted me in oneness with him.

As I stayed there, the burden and the fatigue of this lifetime was lost and in reality–Time stood still. Now that I was here, he blessed me to have a session that would heal me and release me from many unrequired knots that were holding me back from living an enriched life.

Taking his blessings, I (my awarness) travelled to another dimension, place and time. Once again I felt the same feeling like a spinning ball at great speed and I found myself in a lifetime that was energetically holding me back in this life.

I humbly apologise to you for not sharing the details of that life here as I feel the events of that lifetime hold no significance anymore to me or to you. What is more important is what was my learning from that life and how I could free myself from the intense pain of that life which blocked me from living this life to its fullest.

It all came as a movie, I knew I was just witnessing it, and yet I felt overwhelmed with emotions that were so real.My mother from this life, was my mother in that lifetime too and whom I had lost when I was only 6 months old. I shared different relationships with Punit, Bishakha and my brother too in that lifetime.

I witnessed that life till the end and I also witnessed my death in that lifetime. It was such a liberating experience to see my soul, leave its body that had become old and frail.

Once again I found myself in Sai-Baba's company. This time there was no spinning. He was just there as my soul very smoothly left that body.

I find that words, in spite of being such a powerful medium to express, are limited when it comes to explain/describe the intricacy of such transcendental experiences.

I felt light as a feather in weight and at the same time I felt myself as a spark of light. His presence comforted my soul who had just witnessed and felt a turmoil of emotions once again of a lifetime of pain and suffering. For a while I just stayed there in his warm and empowering presence. He then smiled a

loving smile and questioned me with his eyes–
what was my learning from witnessing the
experience of that past life and lesson for this
life?

*The session had cleared all the clouds of
darkness and opened a new horizon of clarity
and understanding of things in the real(true)
sense.*

*It had opened a new door to Spiritual knowledge.
It gave me a real understanding of life, of
journey of a soul, of soul-connections, group
souls and soulmates, of death, of the time in-
between the two lifetimes, of spiritual world, of
spiritual cords, of Spiritual guide.*

Now I could also understand :

*# The need and significance of the loss of my
mother at an early age in this life.*

*It became clear to me that my fear of dying just
like my mother, was nothing but an attachment
to the energy of her death in this life and other
lifetimes that I had lost her. Baba made me see
my soul connection with my mother of love and*

loss. It was a soul contract between me and her that I would lose her in many lifetimes until I learned to let go off the pain of losing a loved one and move on.

With his guidance I agreed to cut that cord of love and loss with her and as I was about to do that I saw her for the last time. Tears rolled down my eyes, as I saw her smiling a heavenly smile. She said :

All is well and will be, love is forever. It is eternal. Just let go...

As I cut the energy cord of love and loss with her, holding Baba's hand I felt her disappear in eternity. It was an overwhelming experience.

 # Next he made me clearly see the reason behind me meeting Punit and choosing him as a partner. We shared the bond of support and friendship in this life and other lifetimes. I agreed to continue with this bond and Baba blessed and anchored this bond.

 # I understood that the deep bond of love that I shared with Bishakha in this life continued

flowing from the love in previous lifetimes. She has been my soulmate and I am beyond happy to know this and feel blessed to have her in this life as well.

 # My relation with my brother suffered in this life because of the deep-rooted hurt that he felt from that life. The supressed anger and pain continued to affect us in this life. Baba summoned the subtle part of him to appear. He seemed reluctant for a bit but then he came. When I asked him the reason for his anger and bitterness, he said it was because I refused to move on with my life after his death in that lifetime and wasted that life in loneliness. It made him angry and he suffered along with me too. I could feel his pain in my heart as he said that. Overwhelmed with love I asked what he would have done, if he was in my place? He replied with immense love in his eyes and said - may be the same! The dam of my emotions seemed to break then, and I was then flooded with tears. Baba took us both in his warm embrace, healed us and liberated us from that Karmic account of unresolved anger and pain.

Love is eternal, and I will love you forever, he said as he disappeared in time and space. We reconciled with each other energetically.

I was in awe of the whole experience. There was a part of me that knew that I was feeling it all at a subtle level and not physical and yet I felt all the emotions in my physical body as well. For the first time I experienced the physical, subtle, and emotional aspects of a soul all together. The biggest realisation I had was that we are all eternal beings, having human experience through this physical body and that the soul never dies. There are so many dimensions to life and existence. Most of us live life with a very limited perception, that we are just a physical body in this physical world. The session gave me a first hand experience of eternity and it was simply spectacular.

The lessons that I learnt for this life were:

#To let go of pain of losing a loved one and to move on.

#. To embrace each moment of life and live and express through life to the fullest.

#To realise the purpose of life and live it.

#To live our life to our best potential, and strive to be the best version of ourself.

#To live and act from the higher self/ true self and interact with all considering their higher self.

Every time we take birth we are born with a purpose, but most often we forget that, influenced by the deep past life samskaras and memories and stuck energies. Frustration, depression, anger, grief, greed, hatred all these are a result of accumulated past life samskaras.

We take birth to clear ourselves of these samskaras so that we can realise our true self and live from our true self which is love, light, peace, joy, bliss, wisdom, power.

But instead of realising our true self we get more and more caught up in the web of material world and start chasing for things, and accumulating things and material wealth calling it search for happiness. So instead of freeing ourselves from the samskaras we accumulate more of them.

As I sat on the bench with me Baba looking at the banyan tree, contemplating on experience I had, I rested my head on his shoulder and felt enveloped in eternal love and peace.

My soul felt rested and rekindled in his presence. I couldn't fully comprehend everything I had witnessed and experienced but I knew a deep healing had occurred. My soul simply desired to be in his divine presence for a little while more...

Finally it was time to get back to the physical world from the subtle world. Baba showered me with his blessings and love. I knew in my heart that this was going to mark a new beginning in my life. In those few hours I had transformed internally. All these years I had felt lost and thought nothing made sense in life, but this experience had brought a paradigm shift in my perception of life. Everything made complete sense now.

It's so easy to sit in a room and crib about life and blame the creator for everything that doesn't seem to be right/favourable to you. It takes efforts and courage to know the Creator. And as you take the first step in your journey to God, you will see he runs to you, taking hundred steps towards you. Why? Because the one who has created us and this world, yearns for our love. Love is the core element of the creation. Then why all these sufferings? Because of free will. In any relationship you would always seek love from the other person out of free will and not out of force. Love can never be demanded or forced upon. It is always given and received freely.

He created us and everything with love, and he is constantly giving his love freely to us, but we are not open to receiving his love. We block ourselves from this everlasting, eternal love and bliss in search of our own identity(ego) not releasing that we are fragments of him. We are his children.

In the beginning I was skeptical to go for the past life regression. There was one side of me that was totally attracted to the idea and yet there was a conditioned mind giving all reasons not to go ahead for such a thing. I had all kinds of fear but somehow I fought those fears, to find the answers to the questions that troubled me. I felt totally blessed and grateful to have had such an experience in life. I thanked the doctor with gratitude and she blessed me to have a happy life. Even today the first glance of my Spiritual master Sai- Baba is as fresh in my memory, as the morning dew.

After coming out of the session which lasted almost three hours, I was in a state of ecstasy. It felt I had just seen a movie, only thing different was I was the lead actor while also watching the movie. It really felt amazing. And I shared all the details with Punit over few days and he helped me understand and process what had happened. He was totally intrigued. Slowly as time passed, the whole experience sinked in and the magic of the healing that happened in that session started to unfold in my life.

I felt a major shift inside me. I felt a new person altogether.

I felt free from all kinds of fears and judgements

and I just simply fell in love with life and existence.

I could now completely surrender to God, all my fears, my guilt, my relationships, my expectations and my life.

Now I started praying to God:

""Dear God I want nothing else but your love. All I want and seek is communion with you. More than anything else I want to live my life in love with you and serving you. Give me the strength my lord, to think, act and be the way you want me to be. With every breath I take I want to feel closer to you and your love."

Eventually, life changed 360 degrees for me and my family. As I let go of my ego to control things in daily life and I let God take control of my life, things started to fall in place so beautifully that I was in complete awe of the beauty of life, and God's ways.

Then one day I came across this wonderful book called -

You can heal your life by Louis hay.

Simultaneously, I came across Dr Wayne Dyer–
one of the Great speakers also considered as
the inspirational Guru in America.

Both Louis Hay and Dr Wayne Dyer had a
profound effect on me and my thoughts. I
completely resonated with what they said and
wrote. It was really strange that being an Indian
I was so inspired by these two foreign figures.
On the contrary I felt; they, their life and their
work inspired love for God and humanity larger
than anything else.

I had a feeling of things unfolding in my life.
The amazing part was that even Punit was
deeply impacted with these two wonderful
personalities and they became our mentors.
Once again, we arrived at the same page in life,
and it was by far the most beautiful page. We
were in complete sync with each other.

We felt new energy in our thoughts, in life,
in our home, workplace and of course it had
a beautiful effect on our daughter, Bishakha.
The metamorphosis I underwent brought
about harmony in other relationships that

had strained in the past few years. The knots of judgement and misunderstanding were beautifully untangled with love and positivity. I reconnected with my Brother and this time he was open and the love and concern I expressed was reciprocated. We gave a brand new start to our relationship and it has only flourished through the years now.

Every aspect of life was now shining bright, as if we were living a magical dream.

When I look back, I recall, that this was the result of passing the chapter of surrender. It is only when I wholeheartedly surrendered to God, that no matter what comes my way I will accept it as his wish for me and look for the highest and best in it. It is then that I was showered with love and positivity and things of the highest and best nature started flowing to us.

SEASON OF COMMUNION

*"When you know how much
God is in love with you,
then you can only live your life,
radiating that love."*

- Mother Teresa

By now affirmations and meditation had become a part of my life.

Every morning, I meditated after my walks (listening to Dr. Wayne Dyer while walking).

After a while in my meditation I started connecting to my higher self. If I had a question, it was answered as a thought. Perfect and crisp answer.

Normally our thoughts go round and round and we know they are ambiguous. It felt weird to me, but as I tried that more, I got answers to my questions. Someday some profound messages. I wish I had made a note of those messages like I do now. Maybe I didn't understand the significance of it then as I do now.

With the way the past life regression session had helped turn our lives around, and opened our horizon to experience life, now even Punit wanted to experience it.

Now that we were liberated from many conditionings, we were more open to exploration in this area.

I looked for a therapist in Ahmedabad. This time amazingly, I came across a contact of a warm looking lady on just dial page Dr. Nair and I called up to inquire.

She sounded like a very warm person on the phone, so, I decided to make an appointment just to discuss the session before actually going for it.

When I went to see her, I intuitively recognised her from some lifetime, just like I had felt about Punit. She felt some connection too. We spent more than an hour talking about so many things revolving around Spirituality, Louis Hay and Dr Dyer, my favourites.

At the end of our conversation she asked me if I knew about the Pranic Healing course, and suggested I go for it.

The next day in my mediation I was guided to go for the pranic healing course. I went for the Basic course the same weekend and in the following six months, I completed 4 levels of Pranic Healing.

Meanwhile Punit did go for a Spiritual Session with Dr. Nair and had quite an experience himself which enhanced his spiritual knowledge with conviction. My father was healed beautifully too by her session. There is something very unique about the hypnotherapy session with Dr. Nair. It is more like a Soul- Healing session, a spiritual session where most of the time one is not taken into a past life, but rather she invokes the Spiritual guides, Masters and Healing angels to directly clean and heal the person.

We learnt that in her intense efforts of raising her consciousness and developing her knowledge in the field of healing and spirituality she was chosen and guided to be a channel for Healing and Cleansing of souls.

The Spiritual masters through her and her guided sessions cleansed and healed the soul's, karmas, the stuck energy, the auras and the chakras, and filled it with Divine love and light and guidance. As much as we were amazed by her sessions, it literally brought about remarkable transformations in us and people who went for the healing sessions with her.

I could actually write a series of books on her and her Healing sessions. They are that divine and magnificent. Not everybody can understand the depth of the healing that takes place in her sessions but only when one educates and opens oneself to the vast ocean of spirituality, that he can understand, to what a profound purpose she has dedicated her life to.

As I did Pranic Healing course, each level left me more and more spell bound and expansion is what I felt. Expansion in wisdom, in knowing and in experience. Even Punit and a few of my cousins went for the course. They all benefited significantly.

All this magic in my life began in February 2016 after I had my PLR session in December 2015.

Each day seemed like a Miracle to me. I lived in Joy and Bliss as I grew more and more in awe of Life and the Creator.

Suddenly from October 2016 I had a recurrent message in my meditations to have a baby. "You must have a baby." I was told.

By now it was confirmed that I was being guided by some higher force/ and not just my higher self. I also connected with Dr Dyer more than once in my meditation. It was magical. Often, I connected to Sai- Baba.

But when I was told to have a baby, I rejected the message completely.

Bishakha had turned 9. With great difficulty I had arrived at this level of "Satchitananda" state of mind and now having a baby would be like going back again to square one.

I had just started to get my body in shape, running, exercising and having a baby would be putting on more weight and added responsibility. Even thinking about it, stressed me.

So, I rejected the message and kept rejecting it for almost 3 months, but the message kept recurring. The more I rejected the recurrent message the more guilty I felt. Finally, one day I discussed it with Punit and he took me by complete surprise by saying that he has had the same thought for a while now and has been avoiding discussing the same with me, knowing that it would stress me.

We were both in awe with this synchronicity. So, we thought of taking help from Dr. Nair. I went to her for a session so that I could get guidance for my spiritual growth and to clearly know if the message that I had been receiving was coming from some higher force or my imbalanced hormones?

As Dr. Nair took me to a deep relaxing state of mind, this time with much ease my awareness reached a plane, where I saw many Spiritual Masters along with Sai Baba waiting for me. Earlier that morning I was told in my meditation- "we are waiting to shower you with our love and gift you the most beautiful thing."

To this day I am in awe of what I experienced in that session. It was confirmed that a soul was wanting to take birth through me. Through

Us - Me and Punit. The soul had been trying to convince me and Punit through recurrent messages in my meditation. But since I had been resistant to the idea, I was led to this session so that with the Spiritual Master's guidance it could seek my permission.

I felt so spell bound by this whole experience. I was in a state of surprise and amazement, the presence of the Masters was so profound that I couldn't deny it. One has to go through such experiences themselves to see for themselves how surreal, yet profound these experiences are. They change you and your lives forever.

I apologised for being so naive to have not listened to the guidance I received in my meditations.

My Life changed that day as I chose to eliminate all resistance.

As I opened myself in allowance for the Divine plan, all the Masters blessed me, protected me, guided me and blessed the soul who was about to begin his journey. Again, I experienced a Miracle, this time it was grander than last time and my faith increased by leaps and bound. I knew, every breath was a miracle in itself and it was just Grace of my Guru that I was so blessed. With every breath then on I was Grateful to God.

I once again surrendered myself completely to God, to work through me the way he chooses to. Such kind of surrender made me feel One with Him. I knew from then on, my life belonged to him. Every breath is his. And I started feeling him all around me. In every one I met, interacted and in everything, I saw. I let his love flow through me, it filled me with infinite peace and joy. The more love I gave out, the more I received and the more I wanted to give out again. I so resonate with Paramhansa Yogananda when he says :

"The greatest romance is with the infinite. You have no idea how beautiful life can be. When you suddenly find God everywhere, when he comes and talks to you and guides you, the romance of divine love has begun."

- Yogananda

I basked in his Love and Light. Now miracles became a daily routine.

A week later, it got confirmed that I was pregnant. Throughout my pregnancy, we experienced many miracles. I will share just a few with you.

One day in my 6th month as I meditated I heard

"Chaitanya , Chaitanya, Chaitanya

I want to be named Chaitanya."

I humbly said to the soul, "so be it"

Google meaning of Chaitanya is –

Divine Consciousness

According to mythology it is the name of Shree Krishna Himself.

Also, the name of the holy saint Chaitanya Mahaprabhu born in Bengal in 16th century who began the bhakti movement and the chanting,

"HARE KRISHNA HARE KRISHNA,
KRISHNA KRISHNA HARE HARE.

HARE RAMA HARE RAMA,
RAMA RAM HARE HARE"

According to the spiritual book, Holy Science by Sri Yukteshwar Maharaj, the word Chaitanya also means the love portion of Divine Consciousness (Kuthasth Chaitanya)

Undoubtedly, I was taken aback and once again my heart was overfilled with joy and gratitude with this experience. I could have never imagined to keep a more befitting name for this child with my limited knowledge.

A part of my limited mind still questioned; how do I know if it's a boy. So, I kept the message to myself except that I shared it with Punit and a very close friend.

I didn't doubt my profound experience but I was certainly in awe of it.

However, the next day what happened is even more magical.

In my yoga class, our instructor usually began and ended the class with two fixed mantras or sutras from Patanjali.

That day after the yoga the instructor had an urge to say a different mantra and since people from all religions came there she apologised in advance, if they have any issue regarding the religious mantra she is about to say...

She asked us to recite the mantra 11 times.

Then she recited,

Om Shree Chaitanya Sainathay Namah (11 times)

By now you can imagine what effect that had on me. This is what the divine does to you once you start walking in his direction. He overflows you with his love so much that everything about life seems to become magical and miraculous and your faith gets stronger with every passing day.

Tears just kept flowing through me while chanting that mantra and I felt immovable, for long after that.

Masters were taking care of every breath and thought of mine.

It was during that time that my brother and father reconciled with each other.After 20 year there was harmony in their relationship which was unbelievable. Both my father and brother were transformed individuals now, a lot of credit goes to the healing sessions of Dr Nair. My prayers for reunion of a family were answered.

I felt so loved once again after all these years as two people that mattered the world to me came together in peace and love. My faith increased in manifolds and God as if kept rewarding me for all the years of love and faith.

My heart was overflowing with gratitude.

I felt so loved and cared for, not only by people around me but by the Creator himself.

I saw this as the Grace of God and the divinity of the baby (soul) inside of me, that brought so much love to me.

Later in my pregnancy my doctor, informed me that she wouldn't be there for my delivery as my due date clashed with her son's wedding in the U.S. She promised me to hand over my case to a good doctor.

She introduced me to Dr. Patel.He was nice

and personable. Just before my due date, in one of my appointments, I casually told him about how exactly I would want my delivery to be that I would like some music and a candle lit and I aimed for natural childbirth and not a C-section. He was impressed by the clarity of my thoughts.

On 31st October I went to the hospital around 9 am with mild contractions.

I was thrilled that finally the wait was going to get over and I was going to hold this miracle in my hand soon. However the whole day went by and the actual contraction began only after 9 pm. In my mind my prayers and affirmations kept playing. It may sound ridiculous, but I meditated twice that day in the hospital.

I was told by Sai Baba, *"you have to be very, very very Strong. It is not going to be as easy as you thought. It is going to be very painful and you have to be strong. A lifetime of karmas is going to be nullified, for him as well as for you through this pain. It is going to be equally difficult for him. So, you have to be strong. You cannot be weak. We are here for you. We will be with you all along."*

I was prepared for what was coming... The labour got stronger and by 3am I had lost all the strength and patience. In that moment of weakness I pleaded for a C-section, however Punit held strong just like during Bishakha's birth. Also the doctor showed extreme patience and supported us to go for a natural birth.

On 1/11/2017, at 5:14 am Chaitanya was born and we rejoiced as this beautiful soul took his first breath by Thanking all the Masters and our Spiritual Guru Sai Baba. The pain my body underwent during his birth is as inexplicable as the beautiful sessions I have had with the Masters.

However I felt their loving presence all around me in everyone and everything. The candle was lit and he took his first breath meditating to the music of I Am, on which I meditated daily. Like Bishakha, Chaitanya was also born with the birthmark of Udi on his forehead.

How much more beautiful a life can get I

wondered! So blessed, so blessed I felt. I was at the peak of my love with God.

It was time to Rest and Rejoice...

Once back home my body quickly started recuperating much to my surprise, after the turmoil it had gone through of an extremely elaborate labour.

I mediated on the 7th day after he was born. The Masters rewarded me:

"We are so happy... that you passed this extreme test of Patience and Faith, so beautifully.

I apologise that I gave up and asked for a c-section.

They said you gave up physical strength but that is when Punit became your Strength.

And not even for a second either of you lost your FAITH.

We were there all the time, all around you in every single thing and every single person around you and in You."

I cried ...

I had felt that Divine presence...

I was so humbled and felt Grateful...

Chaitanya is a beautiful kid. As a baby he just fed and slept, never cried and was always peaceful. Holding him would make you forget everything and you would be consumed by his loving aura and become one with him. His charisma makes us forget everything and makes us simply focus on "Now".

My elder one always knew it would have been a boy. She was overjoyed to have her little brother. There is no greater joy for a parent than to see how magically the siblings bond.

Ever since his birth, Life has had its own course with us. We are always prepared for surprises. Before his first birthday we made spiritual trips to 12 different places in India, without any prior planning. It just happened and kept happening.

On every trip we had many magical and miraculous experiences. We celebrated his 1st birthday at Iskcon temple with kirtan and prasad. It turned out to be Radha Ashtami that day, again we didn't plan ahead, it seemed to happen in an automatic mode.

From the moment I was told in meditation to have a kid and till he was 1 year old; that is approximately 21 months of my life I felt I was so taken over by the divine energy. Everything about me and my life was fictionally peaceful, happy and blissful. Everything flowed in auto mode.

Slowly, the magic seemed to be fading as I wasn't able Meditate and connect to my source everyday.

As he grew and started walking, running around and became naughtier, it got difficult for me to take time out of my routine which now included two kids that I was so unprepared practically, to rear up. At times I found myself incapable of handling things.

I started getting irritable and had my own meltdowns.

Weaning him off made me very vulnerable,

emotionally.

I was on a spiritual high since long, maybe I had to go through the down to make the cycle complete. I felt post-partum hit me by December 2018. I was aware of it; however, I was not able to help myself. I just failed to manage my time, routine and organise everything.

My relationship with Punit was put on a back-front as I was overloaded with the constant care of an infant and somehow we were not able to manage the time to connect with each other. This distance further disturbed my mental state.

I felt more frustrated as I got more and more exhausted on a physical level. I started having frequent meltdowns and once again my relationship with Bishakha suffered.

I felt terrible after every meltdown and I realized that once again I was falling into the trap of negative cycle.

I wondered after having reached this far, how this could happen?

I had no answer. In my heart I knew I had to take time out for myself but it seemed impossible for me. I remembered the last time I meditated, which was when Chaintanya was around 8 months old, I received a message that "You must wake up at 5 am. Great things have to be done now."

I had ignored it because waking up at 5am seemed impossible to me. Something I just couldn't do with the kind of life I was living.

Close to October 2019, I felt a desperate need to meditate and find my peace back again.

I knew if only someone could help me, it was Meditation and my relationship with God.

I started getting up early, compromised a little with the other things and started meditating.

Once again turned to God. But I felt a disconnection, as if something was blocking me.

I felt the need to go to Dr. Nair for a cleansing session and scheduled one. A cleansing and healing of my aura and chakras was done in that session. I was healed of all the Physical pain I felt in my body and negative emotions that were blocking me, to establish my connection with God. The Masters bathed me in their divine love and energised my soul. Once again I opened the door of my soul, for the Divine to flow in. Now I knew things were going to fall in place again and they did.

I continued meditating daily, God and me, we started picking up from where he had left just like old friends do. He is so kind, just waiting for us to open our hearts and he is right there.

Early in December I received a message to invite one of my Pranic healing Instructor home, for dinner. Though I was amazed and wondered why he would come for dinner to our place; when I called to invite him, he readily agreed and promised to come over the following week.

I was excited as once again I could feel the magic of the divine starting to unfold. He came for dinner following week and we had a nice time sharing our stories of magic and miracles that revolved around Chaitanya's birth and after birth stories with him.

In many interesting conversations we had, just half an hour before he left, he mentioned Eileen Caddy from Scotland, and he suggested that I must read a book by her,

"Opening of the doors within."

I very promptly ordered the book the next day and as it arrived I started reading it.

As I read the foreword, I was completely moved. I felt a shift happened in me, as if the purpose of my life was uncovered for me through that book.

I knew with crystal clear clarity what I had to do. All I had to do was take time out for meditation and everything will fall in place. The only thing that interested me in life now, was talking and being with God and for that I had to take time out.

I knew the only obstruction in my way to my purpose now was Me- myself.

All the things I needed to know, all the answers were within me.

Next day, I got up at 5 am and spent time reading the book by Eileen Caddy and meditating. I spent 3 hours in complete peace and bliss. I felt nurtured in the powerful words of God that poured through her and as I read those words I knew that they were reaching out to me, The Masters were waiting for me to surrender as a channel to them so that they could flow in me and through me.

The next day again I got up at 5 am.

I read and meditated upon God. Every Word transformed me, uniting me with the divine. How do I express the magic of those early mornings when God tried to convince me that I could be his channel too. That I had crossed all the barriers of darkness in my mind to have this communion. He had started pouring his Light on me, all I needed to do was be in allowance of this Divine Communion.

I completely believed what was happening and yet it was difficult for me to accept that such a thing could happen to me!

Am I that deserving ? Why me ? there were

questions that bothered me... the whole week no matter what the questions I kept reading and waking up at 5am. How could I not?

After a week, messages started flowing to me like heavenly showers...

I started sitting with a book and pen and the Masters wisdom began to pour in me and through me.

Messages of profound wisdom.

All my questions were answered. All my doubts cleared.

All this while they were preparing me for my purpose.

I had to go through everything I went through, to arrive here.

The magic of those early hours extended during the day. My relationship with Punit started blooming once again. We had so much to share that days ended but our talks didn't seem to end.

Everything started falling in complete

synchronicity.

This book is the fruit of their wisdom. Every lesson taught is by them. They say it is a Co-creation, by them and me.

However, I give them the complete credit of this book, I only decided to show up every morning, and they were there waiting for me.

To pour in me and pour through me.

I feel absolute Joy in serving them and you, by writing this book...

Every day after that has been miraculous for me.

Every day they have helped many people in so many ways through me and through Punit.

Every message I receive in the morning has unfailingly been authenticated in more than one way during the day, so that I wouldn't fall prey to my conscious mind, which is made in a manner that it sees and believes things only from the five senses.

But life is beyond our five senses. The vastness

of Life is beyond one's comprehension.

One needs to meditate, read and upgrade oneself about it. Experiences are much greater than facts.

Every day without fail as I opened myself to them, they shared whatever the need of the day was. I was like a vessel to the cook, just waiting to be used. The vessel has nothing to do with the menu.

This has been my Journey to God until now.

I was told to write my story honestly here without any fear so that each one of you realise that you are loved and protected too. It is not that I am a special child to God. God loves all his children equally. Divine communion is a birth right of each and every one of us.

> *"I have been all things unholy,*
> *If God can work through me,*
> *He can work through anyone."*

- St. Francis of Assisi

He is constantly seeking our love. When we suffer, he suffers too. The feeling of incompleteness we feel, he feels too, without our realization and love. We all know through the various relationships that we are blessed with, that love can only be given out of free will and not any compulsion.

God yearns for our love, but it is our free will to love him. When you choose to love Him, the feeling of incompleteness vanishes and feeling of Bliss and Oneness supersedes.

It is only through communion with God that you can feel eternally complete .(not needing to be, or seek anything else, nothing missing)

I remember as a child I cried out to him so many times in pain and asked -WHY ME? WHY ME?

And today as they choose to flow through me, I ask them again only in tears of happiness and gratitude, Why me?

They answer with so much love-

You chose this path long before you started

this life on earth. You chose this path and you arrived here. We were and are always there with you.

It is always your choice, to choose God or not. He is always there waiting.

Why me, because I Chose him.

I choose Him Every day.

And I request you to Choose Him too.

Each one of you.

If you show up, he definitely will.

Meditate upon God.

Make him your routine.

Choose him Everyday.

Behind the darkness of your ego,

He waits upon you,

To fill you with his

Love and Light.

God Bless You.

LIGHT WORKERS

*"We have been called to heal wounds,
to unite what has fallen apart,
and to bring home those who
have lost their way."*

- St. Francis of Assisi

Once you have realised the true purpose of your Life. Once you have realised that you are his "Light and Love" and you have all his Powers, you arrive to this stage of consciousness where you automatically become a 'Light Worker'.

Now, you no longer can go on with life in a limited, selfish manner. You cannot deliberately hurt others. You rise above all the darkness like stress, worry, fear, jealousy. Now, all you want to do is; Serve. Serve your fellow beings in whichever way you can. You are never tired of helping people all around you, even strangers.

You become like the Sun, who wants to share the Light to one and all without any prejudice. Just like the Light of the Sun brings Life and warmth wherever it falls, you bring Glory wherever you go. You become the messenger, the voice, the hands and feet of God.

You must have come across people in your life, who have this Radiance in their personality. Something about them attracts you instantly.

You feel warm and loved in their presence. Separating from their presence or aura, dulls you and you long to be around them all the time.

All the Holy Gurus, Saints and the Inspirational Teachers and Great People are Light Workers. To name a few, are Sai Baba, Meher Baba, Neeb Karoli Baba, Sri Paramhansa Yoganandaji, Sri Yukteshwar Maharaj Swami Vivekanada, Mother Teressa, Eileen Caddy, Dr Wayne Dyer, Louis Hay and many other, from all across the world.

We are conditioned to put these Great People on a Pedestal and we think that we can never attain great heights like them, or we should not even try to put ourselves along with them. However, if you see, none of these Gurus or saints ever said that I am Great and you are not, so you should worship me. All of these Great people in their teachings insisted on only one thing -

That we are all one, and we are all his children and we are one with him.

To quote Jesus Christ -

"even the weakest among you can do that I do and even greater things"

Humility is the significant attribute of a true Light worker. There are many Light Workers around you and in this world. You need to be aware of them. You are a Light worker as well, who is unaware of his own Light.

The mission of the Light workers is to help their fellow beings to turn within and realise their own Light and, thereby, raise the vibrations of the planet Earth for the Grander and Glorious days to come. A true Light worker is like the Sun, ever Glorious and shining Bright. We are unable to see the Sun during the night because of our limited senses. Sun is always there radiating its Magnificance. We may not be aware of the Light worker's presence, but they are always around us doing their work. Spreading the Light and Love of God.

You may be a light worker yourself trying to realise your own Magnificence, through this book.

So Be it.

From One light worker to another -

Realise that you are His Light and realise your own Magnificence, as you choose to radiate his Light.

In Full Faith and Gratitude,
Zankhana.
A Light Worker.

SOME OF THE PROFOUND MESSAGES FROM THE MASTERS

You need to arrive to a state of mind where
'Everything is fine;
Everything is Good.'
There are no mistakes in the Divine flow.
Everything is fine and Good.

*****

"Be the Light,
See the Light,
Behold the Light"

*****

Everything about the world will seem challenging until you surrender to me completely. Give me all your thoughts and actions; give me whole of you and I will make your path smooth.

I am the doer and the done. Keep chanting my name. In my name there is Glory. This glory will burn your Karmas and bring you closer to me.

*****

You can take that much nectar of life; as much as you wish...

It is endlessly sweet.

If you seek more; you receive more.

*****

All the obstacles are in your Mind. See with clarity and there will be no obstacles at all. Everything is/was/will always be in Divine order. So why worry?

Surrender all the time not just sometimes.

Until you surrender all the time, there will not be Peace. More peaceful you are the better your Spiritual Growth.

When the Ocean is wild the ship is at risk and the Journey seems treacherous.

Calm ocean with normal waves is what one

looks for in a Journey.

*****

Do not look for me in just temples.

I am inside of you; within you.

Sometimes look for me within and you will find the treasure of my Presence deep within you.

God bless you!

*****

Do not judge people and do not judge life from the events happening outside of you.

Look within and see from within.

All the noble work and cleansing needs to start from within.

Start from there.

First you have to turn within yourself, only then you can bring about the change you wish to bring outside. Even when one person turns within, there is a shift in the vibrations of earth. Can u imagine how it works...?

*****

With every soul getting God realised, it is a

victory of Creation, that is what Creation yearns for...

For realising its own GLORY

You do not have to be a Candle.

You are a Sun, each one of you.

Be like a Sun not candle.

Do not burn yourselves to give light.

Realise You are Light and

Radiate Your Light like the Sun!

*****

Everything about life is magical once you turn your awareness inwards.

The troubles the chaos you see outside in your world is a reflection of the chaos within people

*****

All your question will be answered in peace...

All your worries will dissolve in peace...

All your joys be elevated in peace...

For silence is the key to living a blissful Life...

Silence is the Language of God.

Peace be everywhere, in and around you.

*****

Realising God is only the threshold,
Living a Realised life is what human - life is all about.

*****

Divine is the soul, that aches in other soul's pain.

Divine is the soul, that smiles at other soul's joys and success...

Divine is the soul, that yearns to give out of love...

Divine is the soul, that pines and strives for God's love and light

Divine is the soul, that spends his life in singing lord's praise...

Divine is thy soul,

Divine is thy soul.

Blessed thy be.

Blessed thy be.

*****

EPILOGUE

I am really Grateful to the Masters for choosing me to be a part of this amazing book.

Being Zankhana's soul mate, I have had the fortune to see her entire transformation very closely. The journey of how a wandered soul makes it to the state of realization and how her individual journey, inspires and leads everyone around her including myself, towards the light.

I met this beautiful soul in the year 2003, at one of the malls in Ahmedabad. Series of events at the mall made us acquainted with each other. In a very short time, we became the best of friends. Her pure heart with love for everyone had a magnetic effect on me. I felt as if I knew her from past lives and soon proposed her to spend this life too. She readily agreed and we got married in 2006.

Whenever I look back, I still find it hard to believe how the universe divinely orchestrated everything in our life and how two complete strangers in the gross world got tied in a nuptial knot, to evolve spiritually together.

As a child being more left brain dominant, I only believed in science, not GOD. I was living an ego - driven life, and would literally debate on anything with logic and scientific outlook. The elders in my family always insisted upon me to join them for daily worships and rituals, but I was never interested. God did not exist for me then. I only believed that it is goodness alone that can make this world a better place.

Soon after my marriage, some of the emotions I felt and realizations that dawned on me cannot be described in words or can logically be explained. I failed to understand those beautiful feelings with my limited brain. These experiences shifted something in me, which was hard to comprehend at the time.

One night, a thought came to my mind. My wife

and I shared a great relation and understanding after few years of friendship and commitment towards each other. I realized how two people in the physical world cannot make a bonding without investing time in each other. That raised a question in my mind, that how can one claim to know God (if any) or feel the bond with Him, who is invisible to us, without making efforts to know Him.

We decided to explore different paths to quench our thirst in search for God. It is only in this process that we started reading many ancient scriptures and holy books full of divine wisdom. It completely transformed us from within.

Many spiritual masters and saints have reincarnated in this world time and again to guide us towards the purpose of our life through self realization, to raise the vibration of our planet earth by uplifting the overall consciousness of the human race.

Fortunately for us, all these happened very organically. At every stage in the process, by reading books and through meditation, as the layers of ignorance were shedded one by one, the embedded divine wisdom came to surface. It took us almost 15 years to reach this stage of awakening.

The current scenario of the world is completely different in this digital age. I sometimes feel that world is not only seeing the advancement in technology but also human beings have evolved in some more techno - human species.

On one hand where we are proud to invent the most advanced gadgets & robots assisted with artificial intelligence, on the other I feel we have been losing the inherent human intelligence with a core natural sensitivity towards nature, animals, birds, eating habits, family bonding, brotherhood, respect, love & the list goes on.

We are getting so engrossed in the gross world that we have almost forgotten our true self, who has taken birth for a far greater reason.

As the time is progressing, world is also changing rapidly, but unfortunately not evolving into a better world.

We are now teaching our children to be

competitive, but not guiding them how to think, what to think, & power of thoughts. I believe one's choice of thoughts, makes one's destiny. Right from childhood, kids are learning to run away or run for things. By the time they grow up, they are in a habit of chasing everything - best grades, jobs, success, wealth, so on and so forth. In chasing all of this, the truth of life and its divine purpose is lost somewhere. This may not be true for everyone but it is true for a majority of generation. There is no sense of fulfillment even after achieving their dreams. There is no joy of living. We have not learned 'Power of Now' & living in the moment.

We have been running on an auto pilot mode, so much that we have lost the patience to read these valuable ancient books meant to lead our path towards the ultimate destination.

We have been living a surrendered life since many years, where in we just pray to God, to help us serve to the purpose that we are here for.

This book, 'Living in light' is the result of the same. The book is wonderfully written by the

Great Masters from the other dimension, using Zankhana as a medium.

This book is intended only to scratch the surface of our core, which may not be currently aligned to the source. It is written in crisp and short chapters for easy read. It will just touch the topics far enough for one to dig deeper to the roots. It will intrigue one to introspect within and break the life-long habit of superficial learning. It has a unique method to reinforce soul's inherent attributes.

This book will help one to open the door within.

Reading this book and being a part of it is a great honor for me. I am genuinely humbled by the Master's Grace in our life.

This book will definitely help you become a better human being. Let us all contribute towards making this world a better place for all of us to live in together with harmony and love.

With Love and in Light,
Punit Tambi

MY INSPIRATIONS

*"You can either be a host to God,
or hostage to your ego. It is your call."*

- Dr. Wayne Dyer

"*I choose to make the rest of my life,
The best of my life.*"

- Louis Hay

"Don't force anything.
Let life be a deep let go."

- Eileen Caddy

ABOUT THE WRITER

Zankhana, is a simple person with a cheerful personality. She believes somewhere deep down in her soul she can still resonate with a child who thinks that happiness is in the little joys of life, like eating an ice cream on a hot summer day, riding a bike or dancing/walking in the rains.

Now a mother of two beautiful, divine children, she lives in Ahmedabad with her family. Born and brought up here, she has a great affinity for her city.

Having been fond of reading since childhood, she always had a desire to become a writer. Little did she know that one day she would become the writer of God, spreading His message .

She feels deeply humbled and grateful as the divine flows through her every morning when she sits for meditation in allowance.

Overwhelmed by their love and grace, when she thanks the Masters, time and again for choosing her for this monumental work, they tell her -

"You chose us and

each one of you can.

The choice is always yours."

Connect with Zankhana @

Zankanatambi.com

20lightworker@gmail.com

List of few books that Changed the course of our life...

- Sai Satcharitra - Life and teachings of Sai - Baba by Hemandpanth Dabholkar
- The Laws of The Spiritual Worlds - Khorshed Bhavnagri
- Many Lives, Many Masters - Dr. Brain Weiss
- Same Soul, Many Bodies - Dr. Brain Weiss
- Through Time Into Healing - Dr. Brain Weiss
- Miracles Happen - Dr. Brain Weiss
- Glimpses of Eternity - Raymond Moody
- Life after Life - Raymond Moody
- A world Beyond - Ruth Montgomery
- You Can Heal Your Life - Louis Hay
- Life Loves You - Louis Hay
- You Can Heal Your Body - Louis Hay
- Living an Inspired Life - Dr. Wayne Dyer

- Real Magic - Dr. Wayne Dyer
- The Shift - Dr. Wayne Dyer
- Co - creating at its Best - Dr. Wayne Dyer &Abraham Hicks
- Ask And It Is Given - Esther and Jerry Hicks
- The Law of Attraction - Esther and Jerry Hicks
- The Vortex - Esther and Jerry Hicks
- Dying To Be Me - Anita Moorjani
- What if this is Heaven? - Anita Moorjani
- Wisdom of The Ages - Dr. Wayne Dyer
- Power of Intention - Dr. Wayne Dyer
- Wishes Fufilled - Dr. Wayne Dyer
- Memories of Heaven - Dr. Wayne Dyer
- Your Sacred Self - Dr. Wayne Dyer
- Change Your Thoughts, Change Your Life - Dr. Wayne Dyer
- The Four Agreements - Don Miguel Ruiz
- I Can See Clearly Now - Dr. Wayne Dyer

- Manifest your Destiny - Dr. Wayne Dyer
- Conversations With God - Neale Donald Walsch
- Conversations with Babaji - Master Pallavi
- As a Man Thinketh - James Allen
- Beyond The Mind - Master Choa Kok Sui
- Possible Miracles - Master Choa Kok Sui Master Choa Kok Sui
- The existence of God is Self - evident - Master Choa Kok Sui
- Ancient Science and Ar of Pranic Healing - Master Choa Kok Sui
- The Spiritual Essence of Man - Master Choa Kok Sui
- Advanced Pranic Healing - Master Choa Kok Sui
- Pranic Psychotherapy - Master Choa Kok Sui
- Achieveing Oneness with The Higher - self - Master Choa Kok Sui

- I AM That - Nisargdatta Maharaj
- Be Here Now - Ramdas
- Miracles of Love - Ramdas
- Be Love Now - Ramdas
- The Divine Reality
- The Impersonal Life - Joseph S Benner
- Tao te Ching - Stephen Mitchell
- God Speaks - Meher Baba
- Meher Baba Discourses
- Autobiography of a Yogi - Paramahansa Yogananda
- Journey to Self - Realisation Paramahansa Yogananda
- Inner Peace - Paramahansa Yogananda
- The Divine Romance - Paramahansa Yogananda
- How to live Wisdom - Paramahansa Yogananda
- *And the list goes on...*

Made in the USA
Las Vegas, NV
26 February 2021

18652345R10104